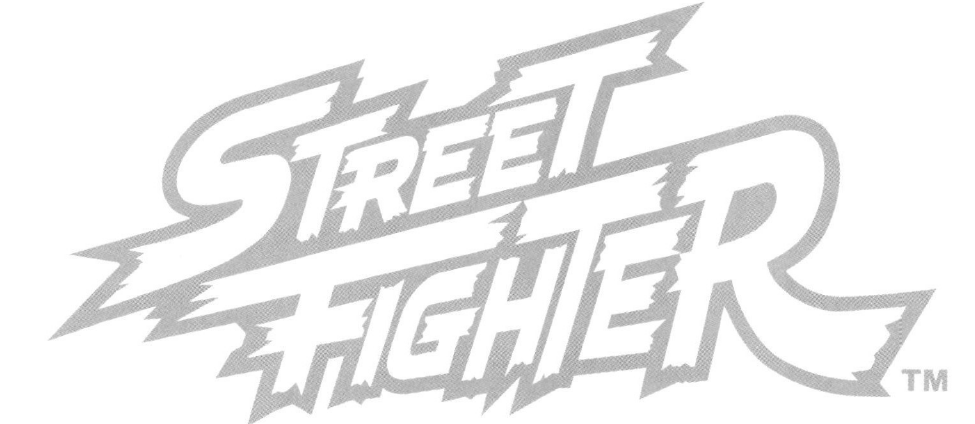

ULTIMATE ART PORTFOLIO

RYU
ILLUSTRATED BY JO CHEN

SAKURA
ILLUSTRATED BY JO CHEN

KEN
ILLUSTRATED BY JO CHEN

FEI LONG
ILLUSTRATED BY JO CHEN

GUILE
ILLUSTRATED BY JO CHEN

DHALSIM
ILLUSTRATED BY ARNOLD TSANG

CHUN-LI
ILLUSTRATED BY JO CHEN

ROSE
ILLUSTRATED BY JO CHEN

MENAT
ILLUSTRATED BY PANZER

SAGAT
ILLUSTRATED BY ARNOLD TSANG

BLANKA
ILLUSTRATED BY JOE VRIENS & CHRISTINE CHOI

F.A.N.G
ILLUSTRATED BY PANZER

RASHID
ILLUSTRATED BY PANZER

VEGA
ILLUSTRATED BY JO CHEN

C. VIPER
ILLUSTRATED BY ADAM VEHIGE

M. BISON
ILLUSTRATED BY JO CHEN

E. HONDA
ILLUSTRATED BY SVEN

AKUMA
ILLUSTRATED BY ARNOLD TSANG

JURI
ILLUSTRATED BY ARNOLD TSANG

EVIL RYU
ILLUSTRATED BY JO CHEN

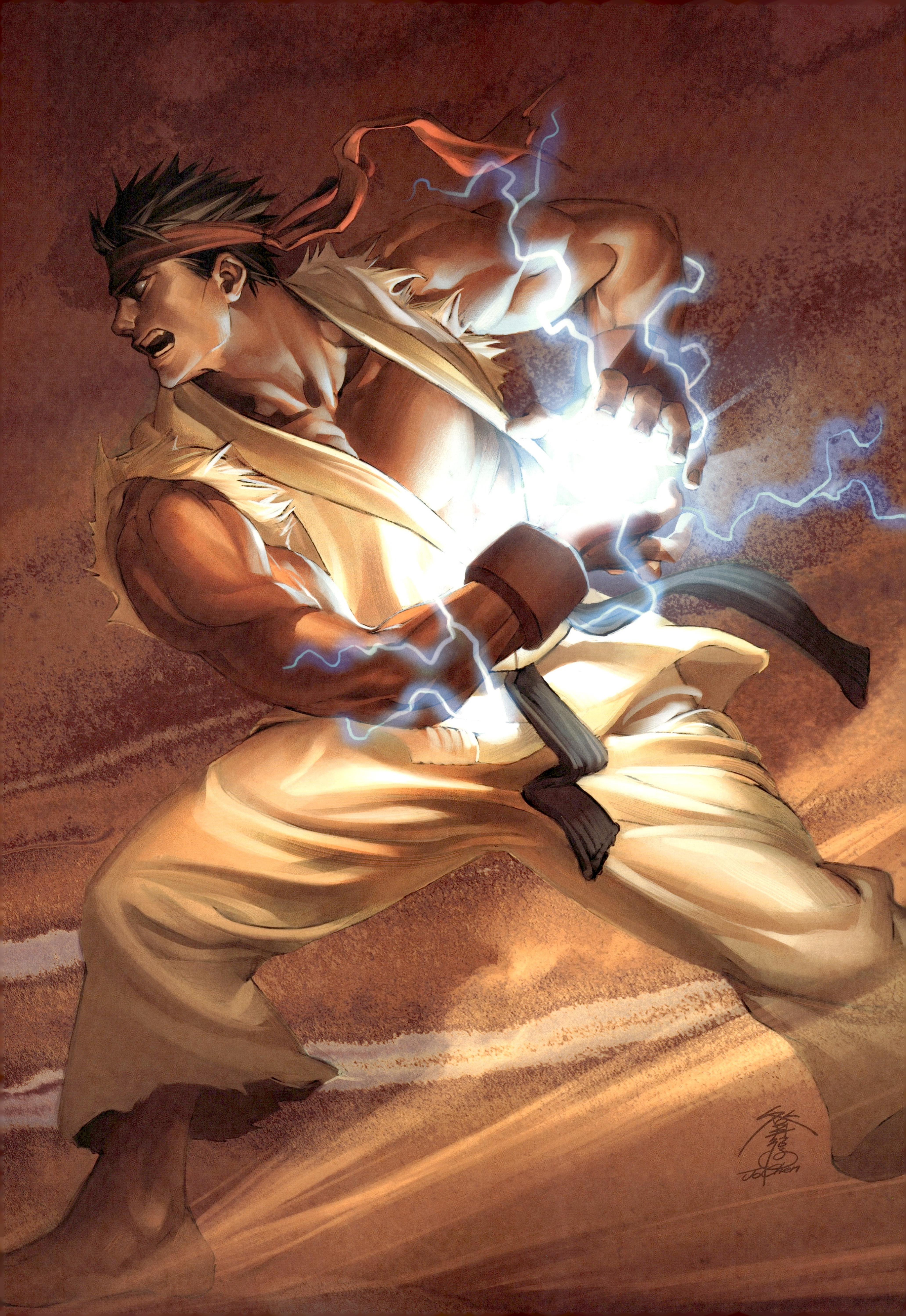

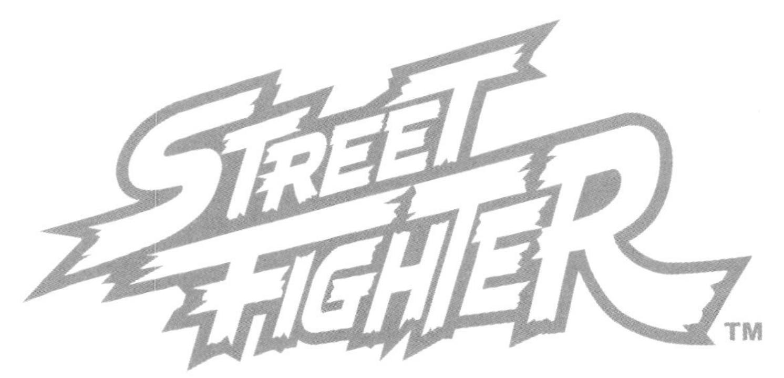

RYU

ILLUSTRATED BY JO CHEN

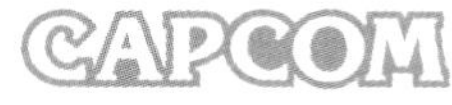

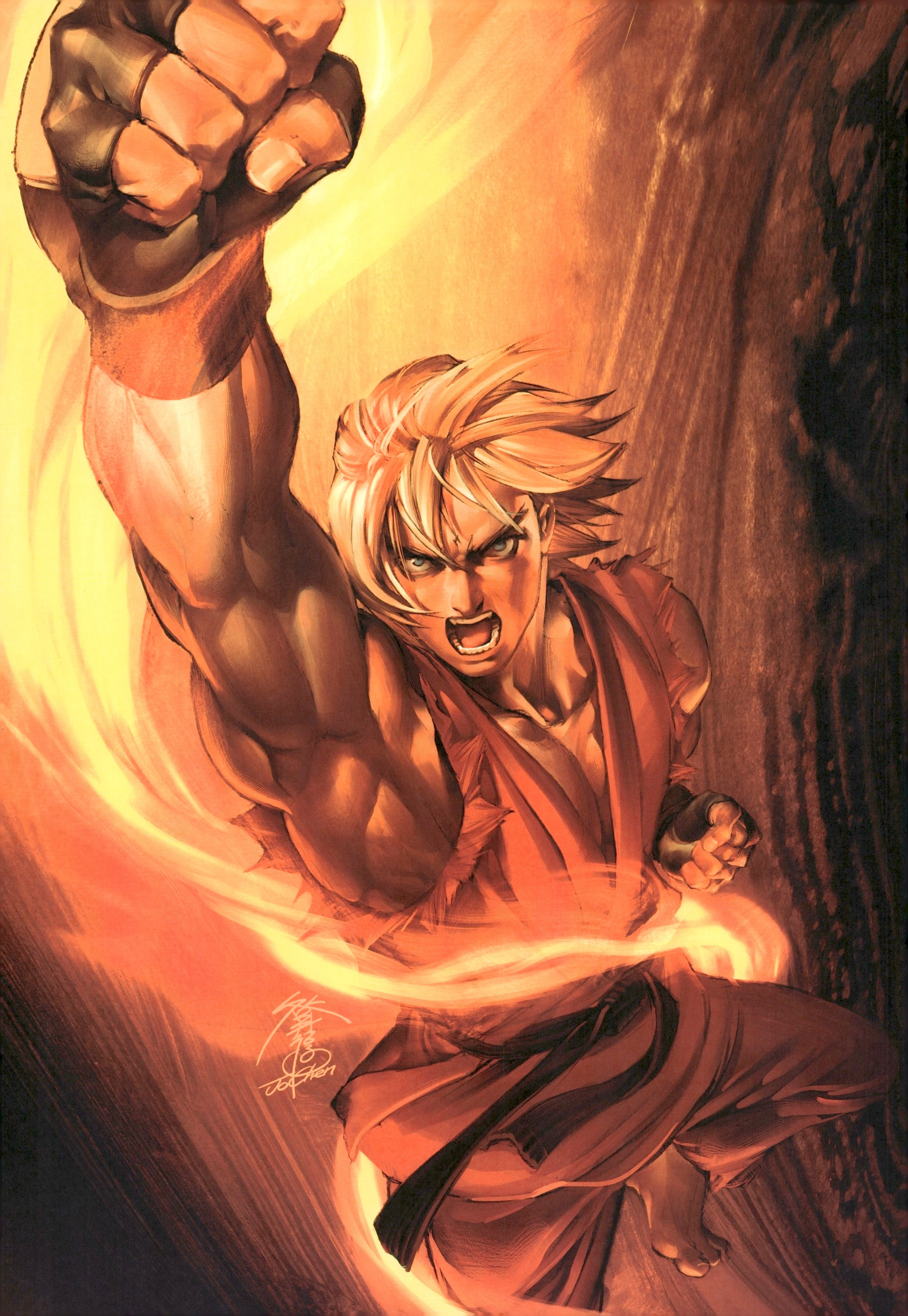

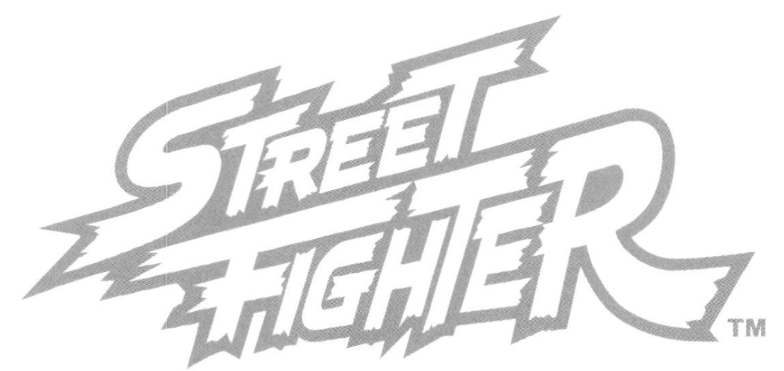

KEN

ILLUSTRATED BY JO CHEN

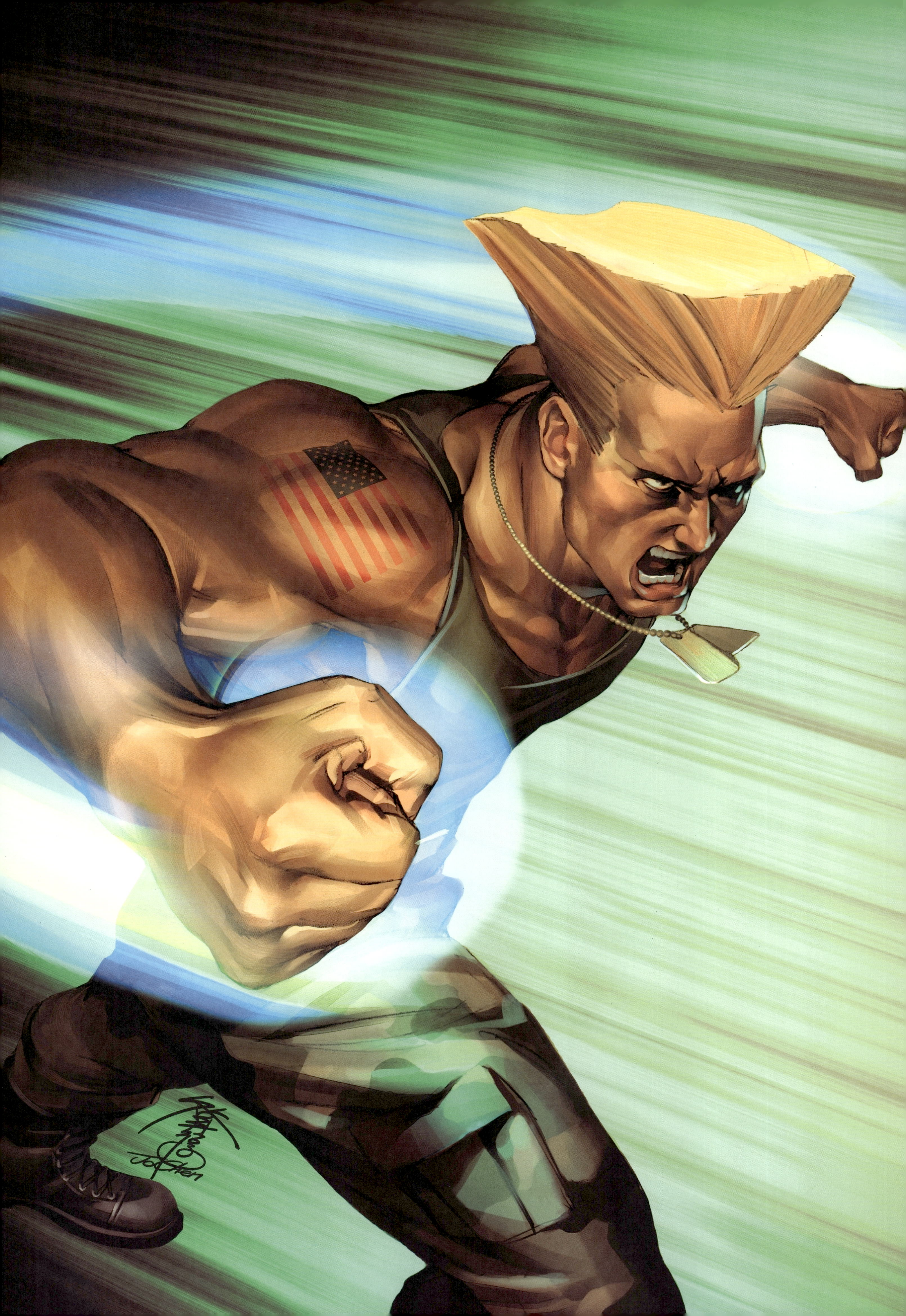

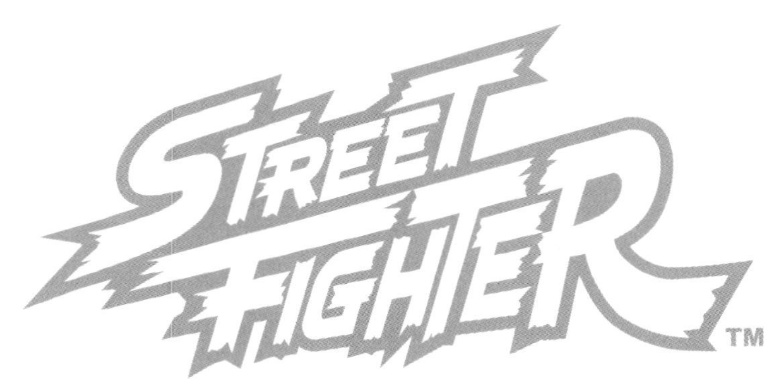

GUILE

ILLUSTRATED BY JO CHEN

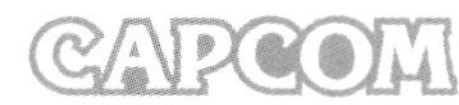

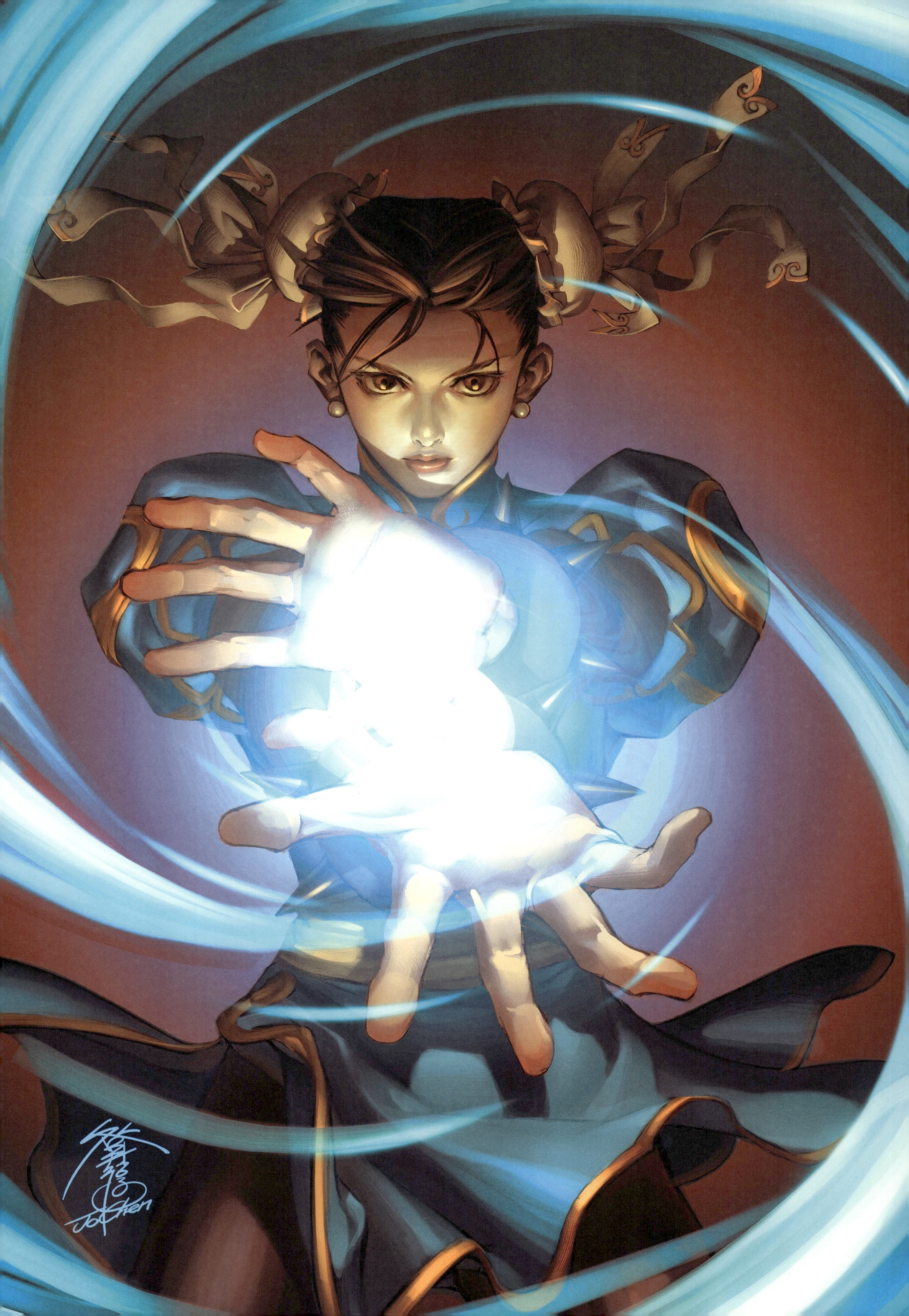

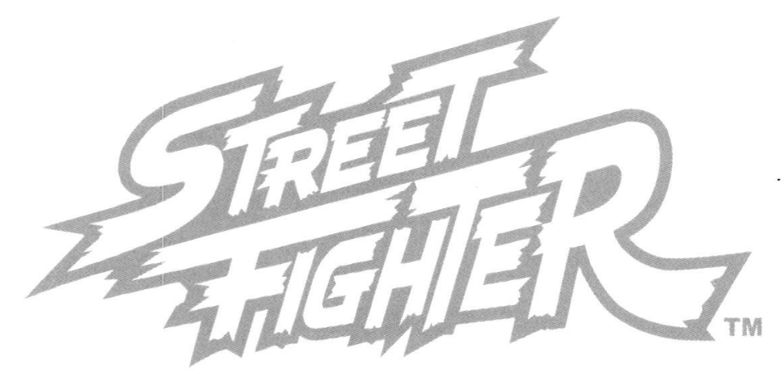

CHUN-LI

ILLUSTRATED BY JO CHEN

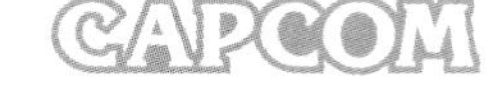

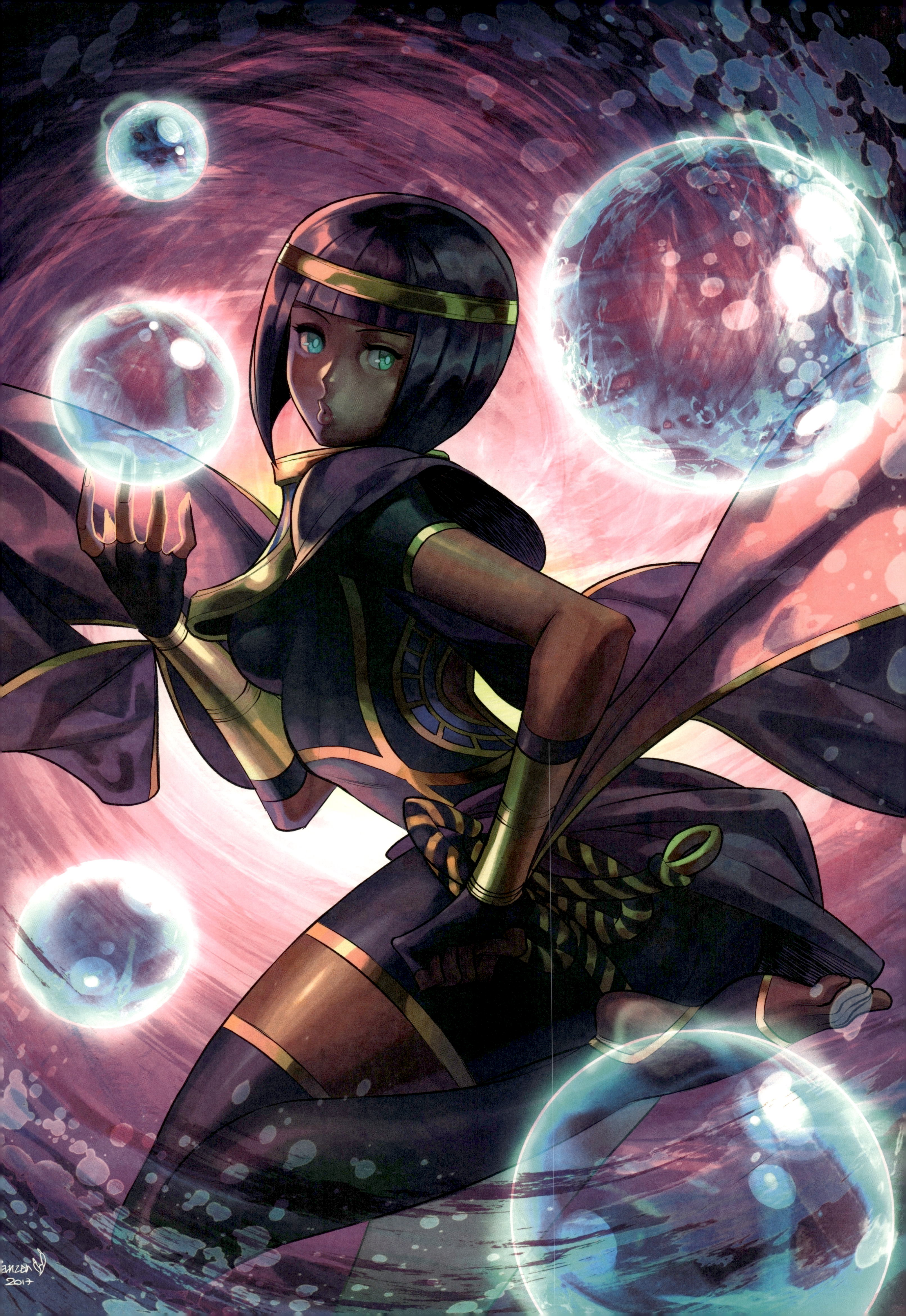

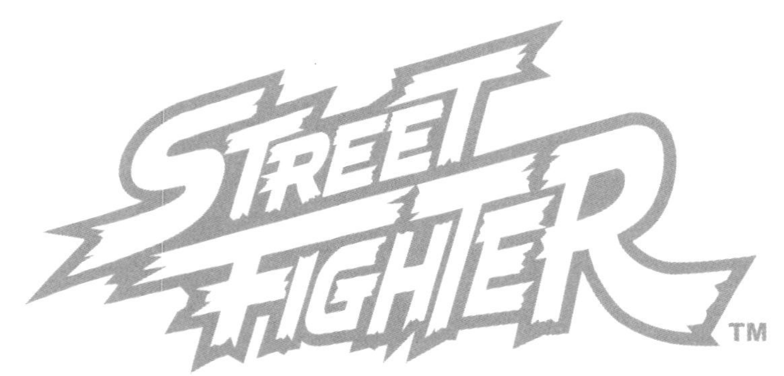

MENAT

ILLUSTRATED BY PANZER

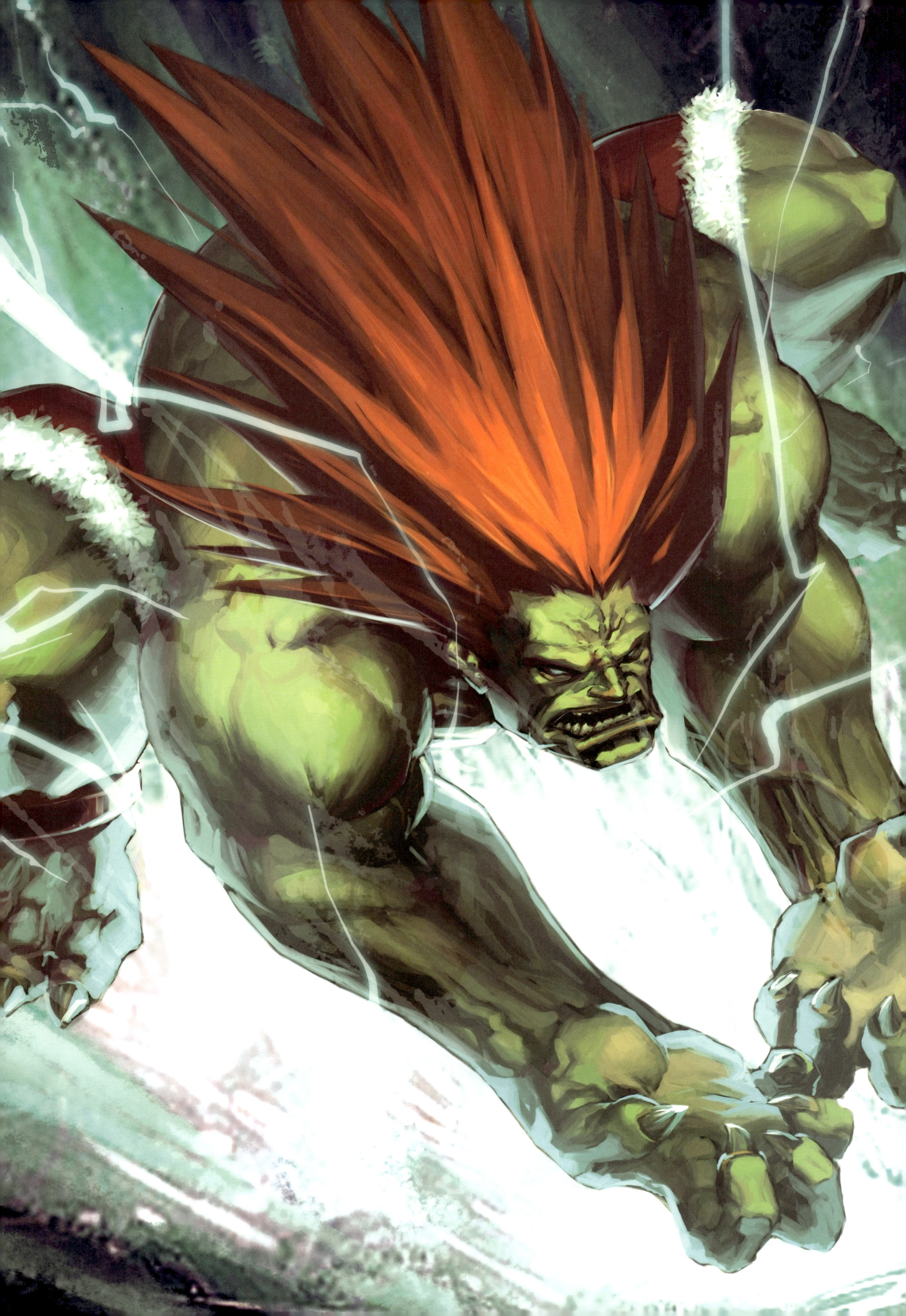

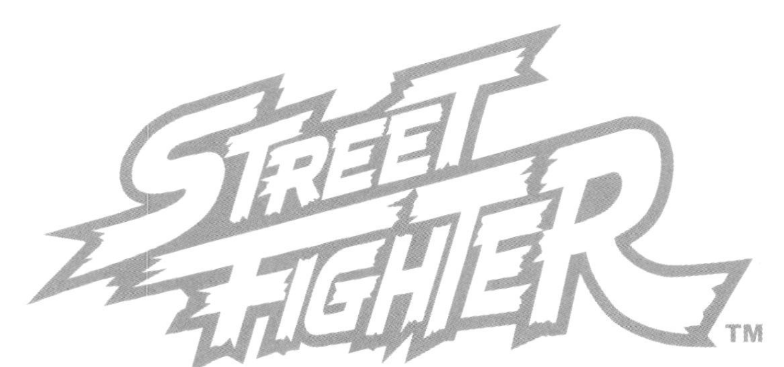

BLANKA

ILLUSTRATED BY JOE VRIENS & CHRISTINE CHOI

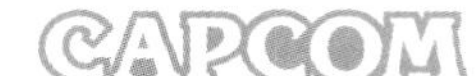

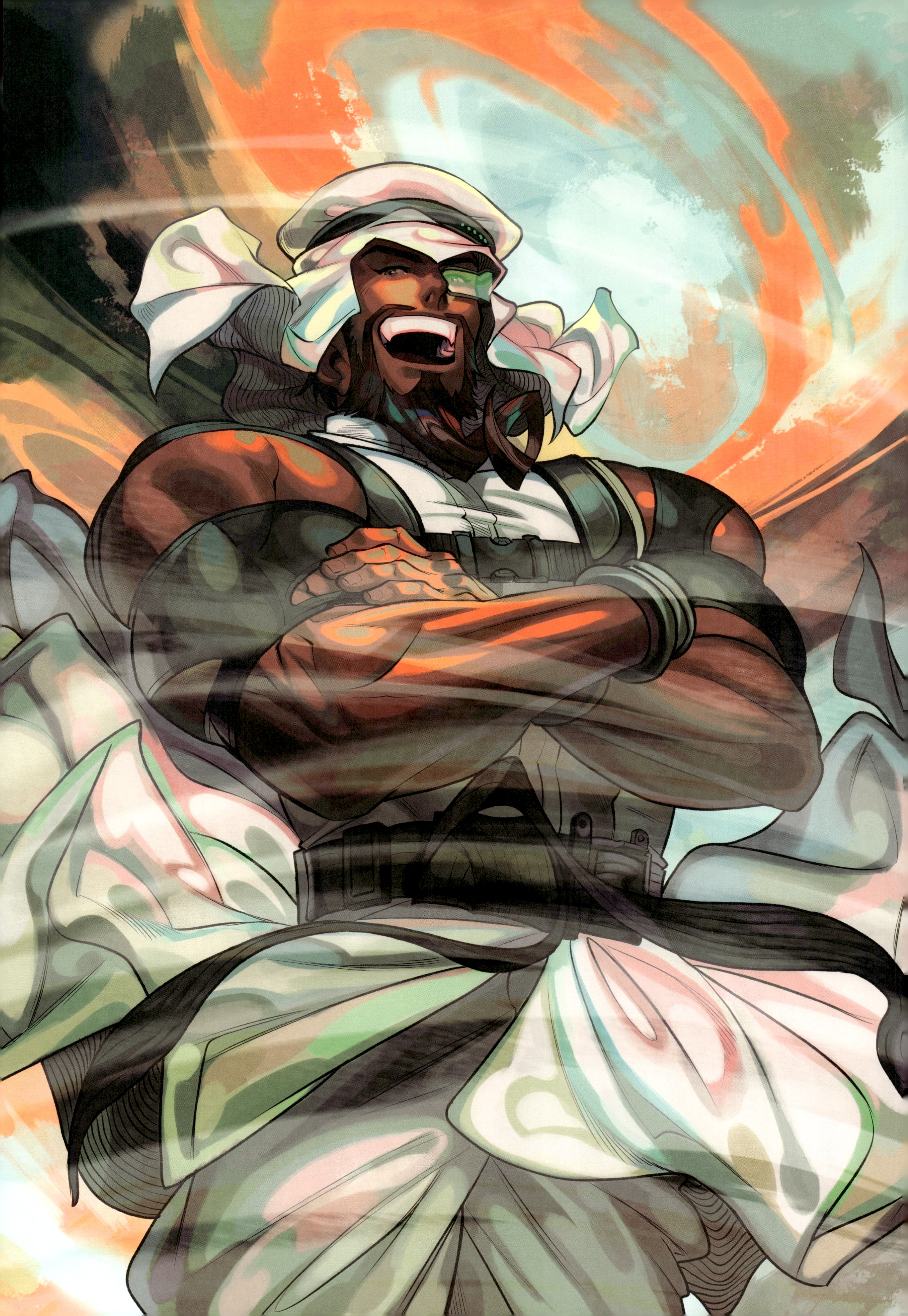

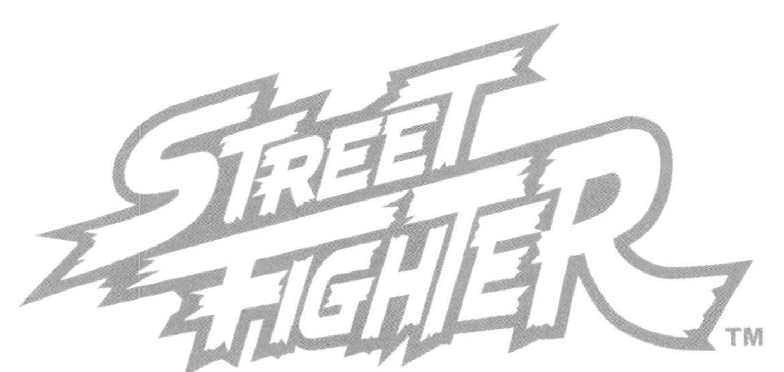

RASHID

ILLUSTRATED BY PANZER

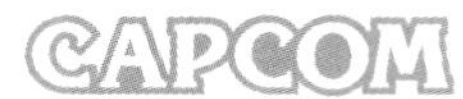

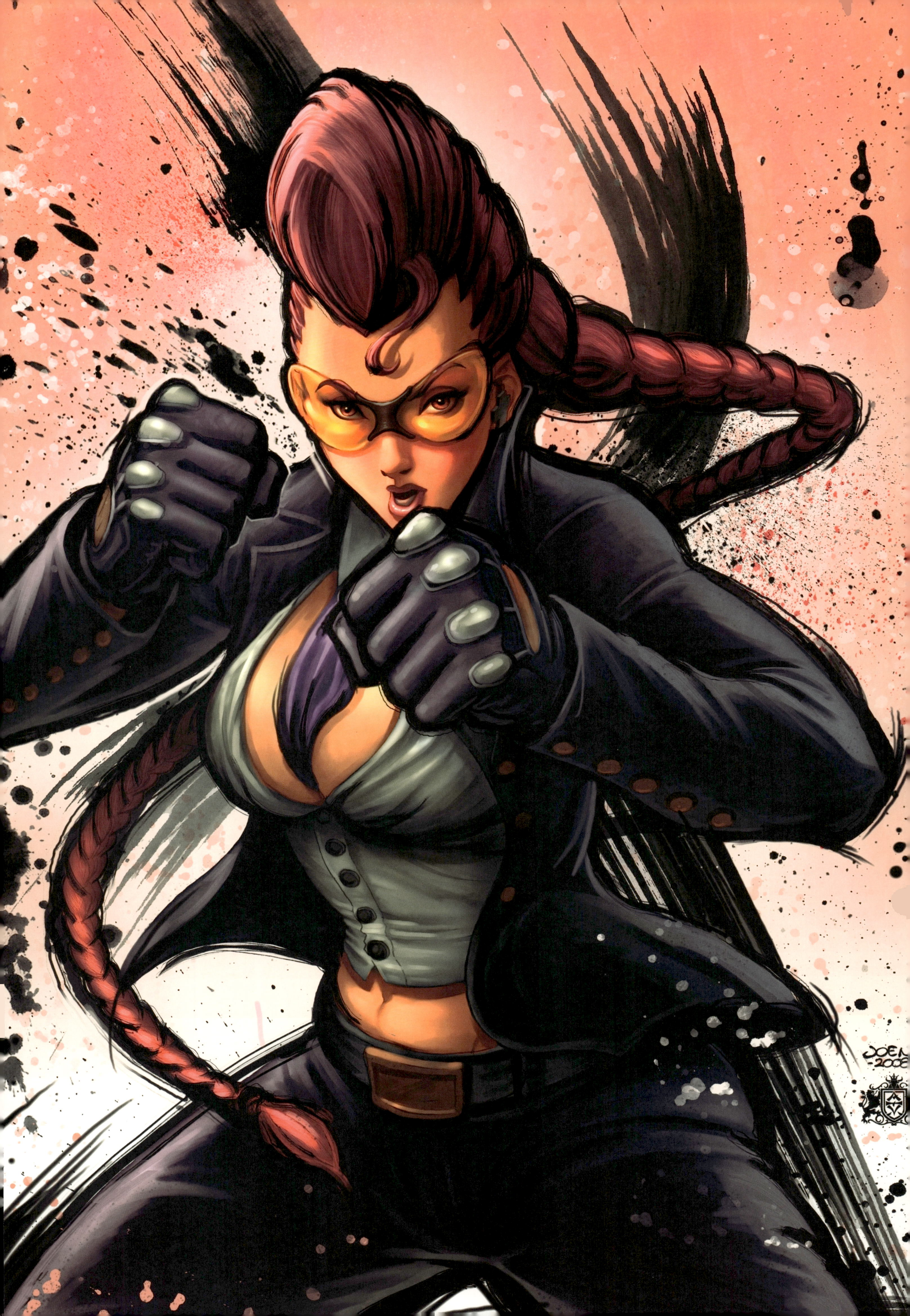

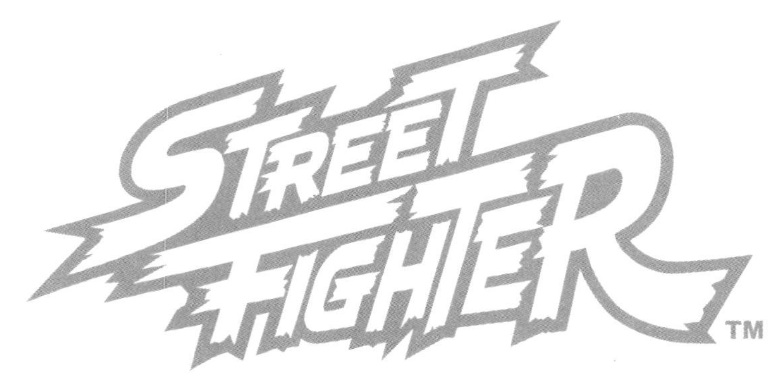

C. VIPER

ILLUSTRATED BY ADAM VEHIGE

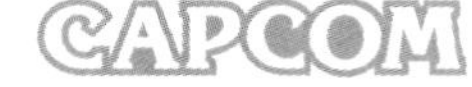

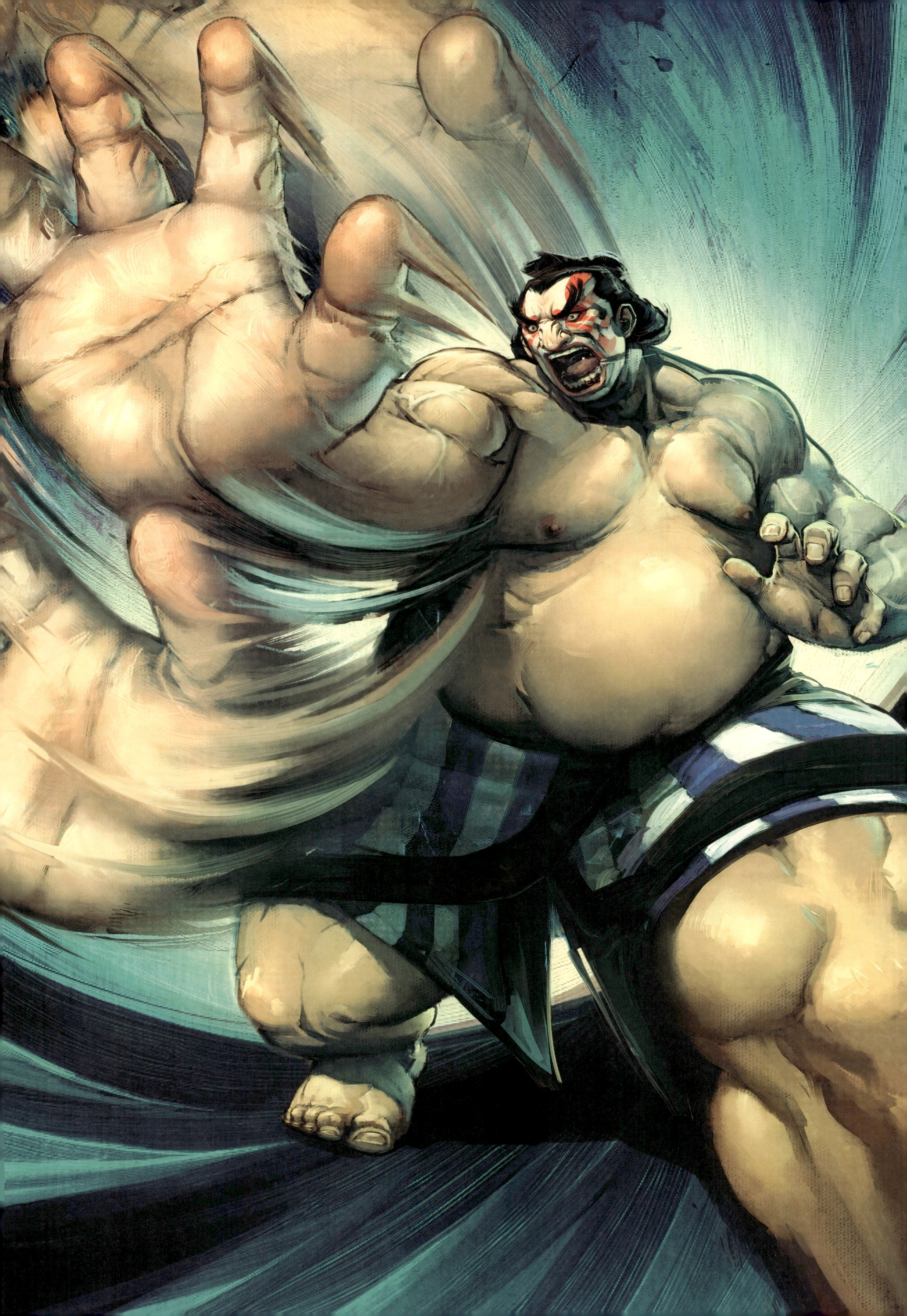

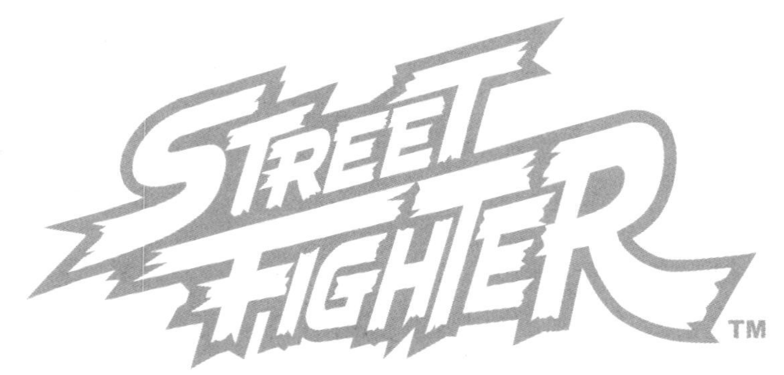

E. HONDA

ILLUSTRATED BY SVEN

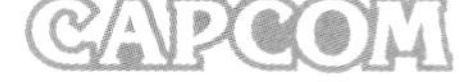

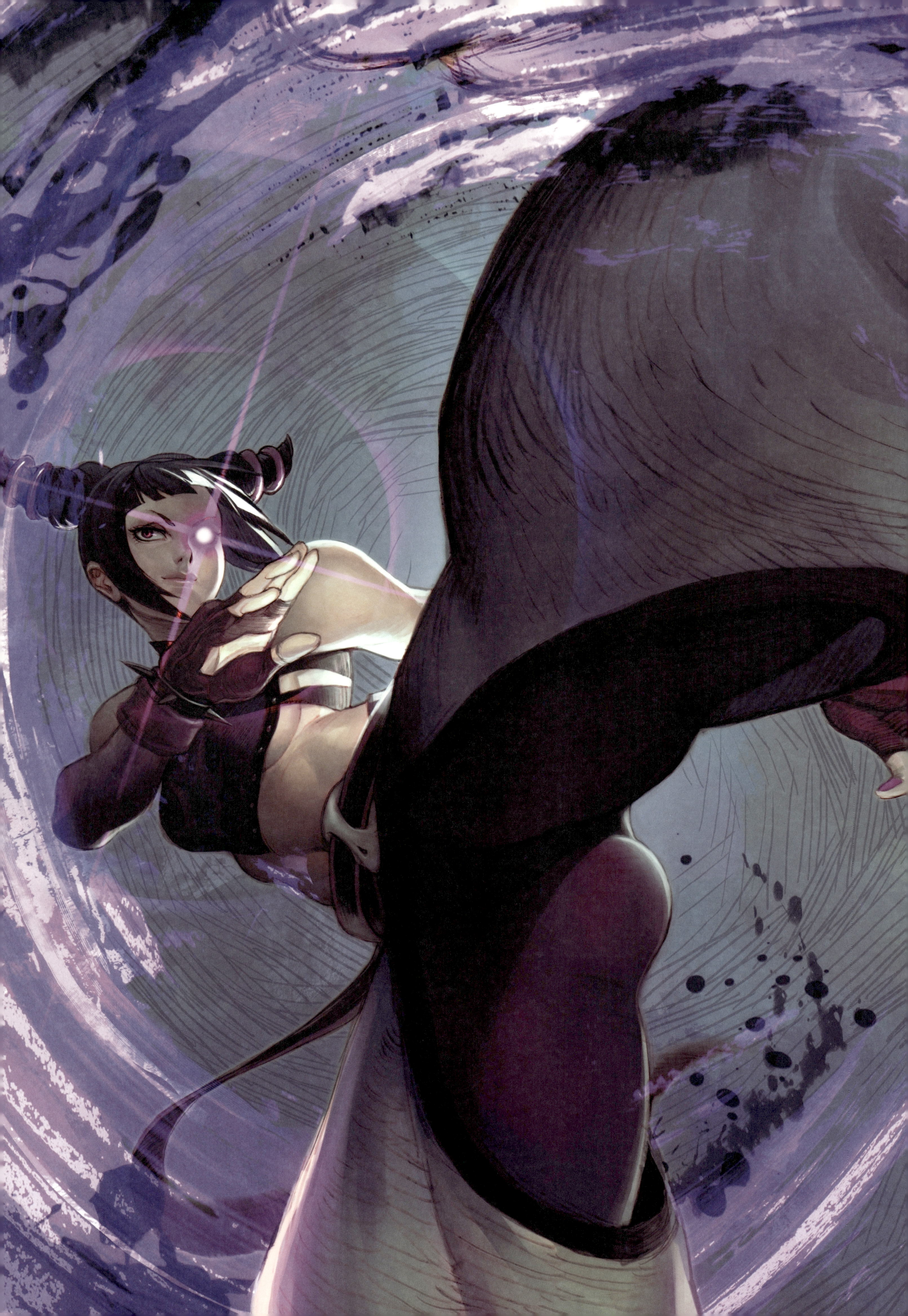

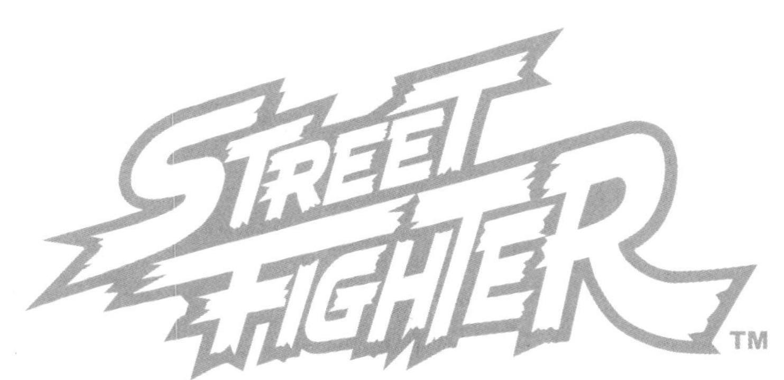

JURI

ILLUSTRATED BY ARNOLD TSANG

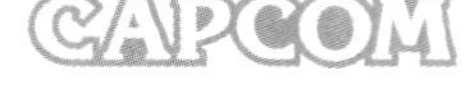

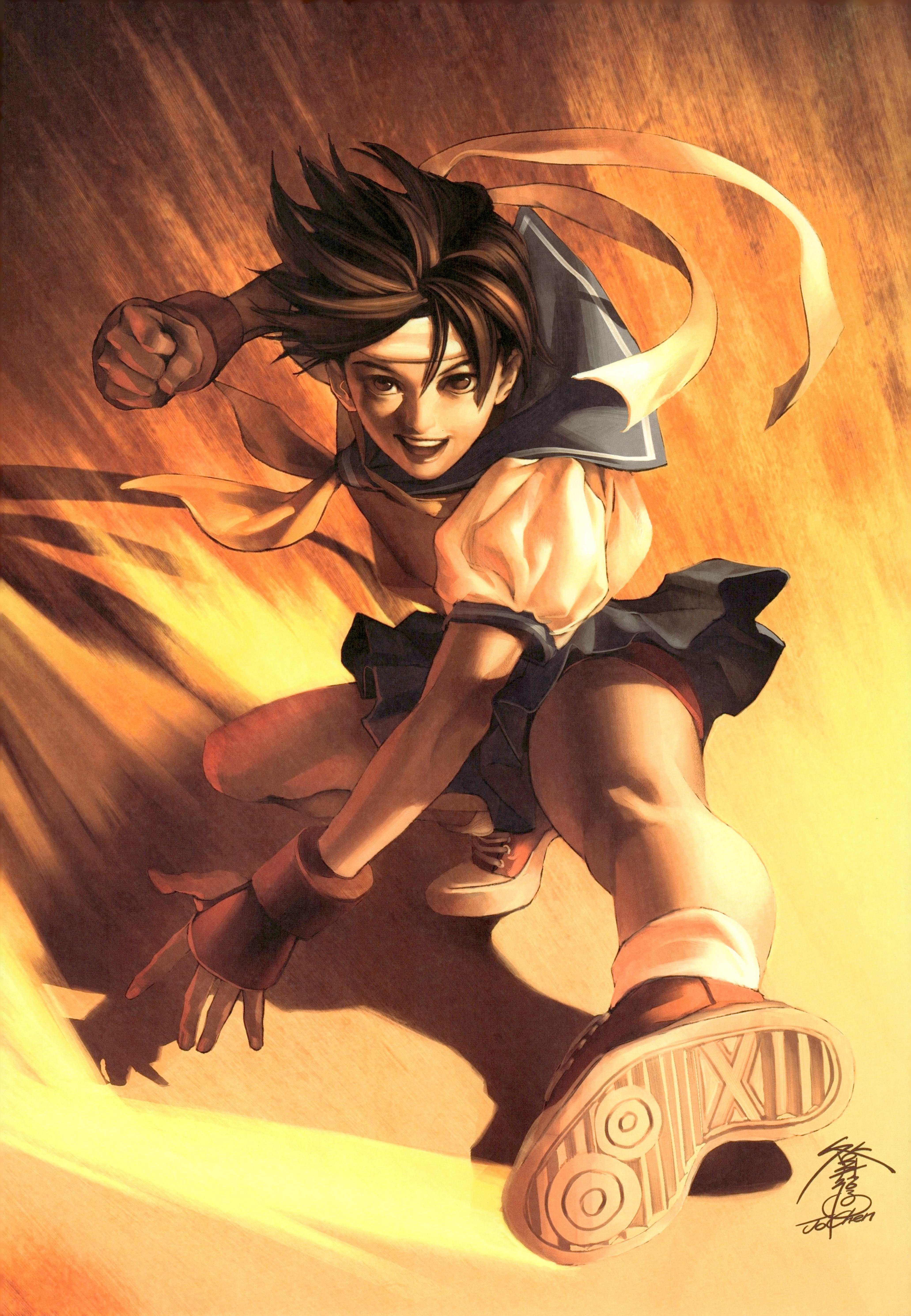

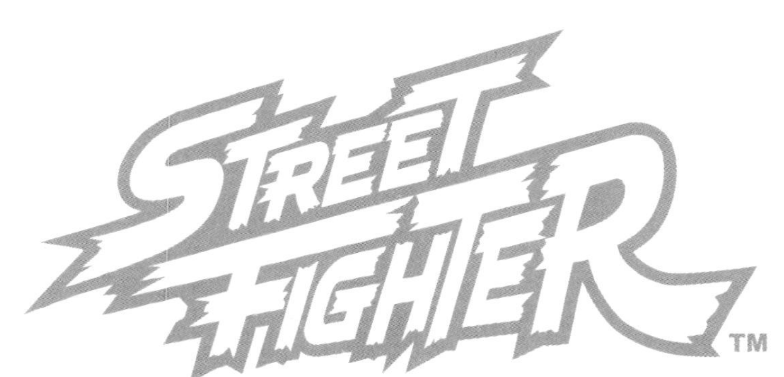

SAKURA

ILLUSTRATED BY JO CHEN

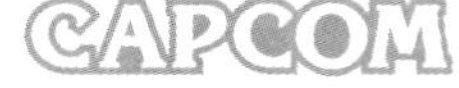

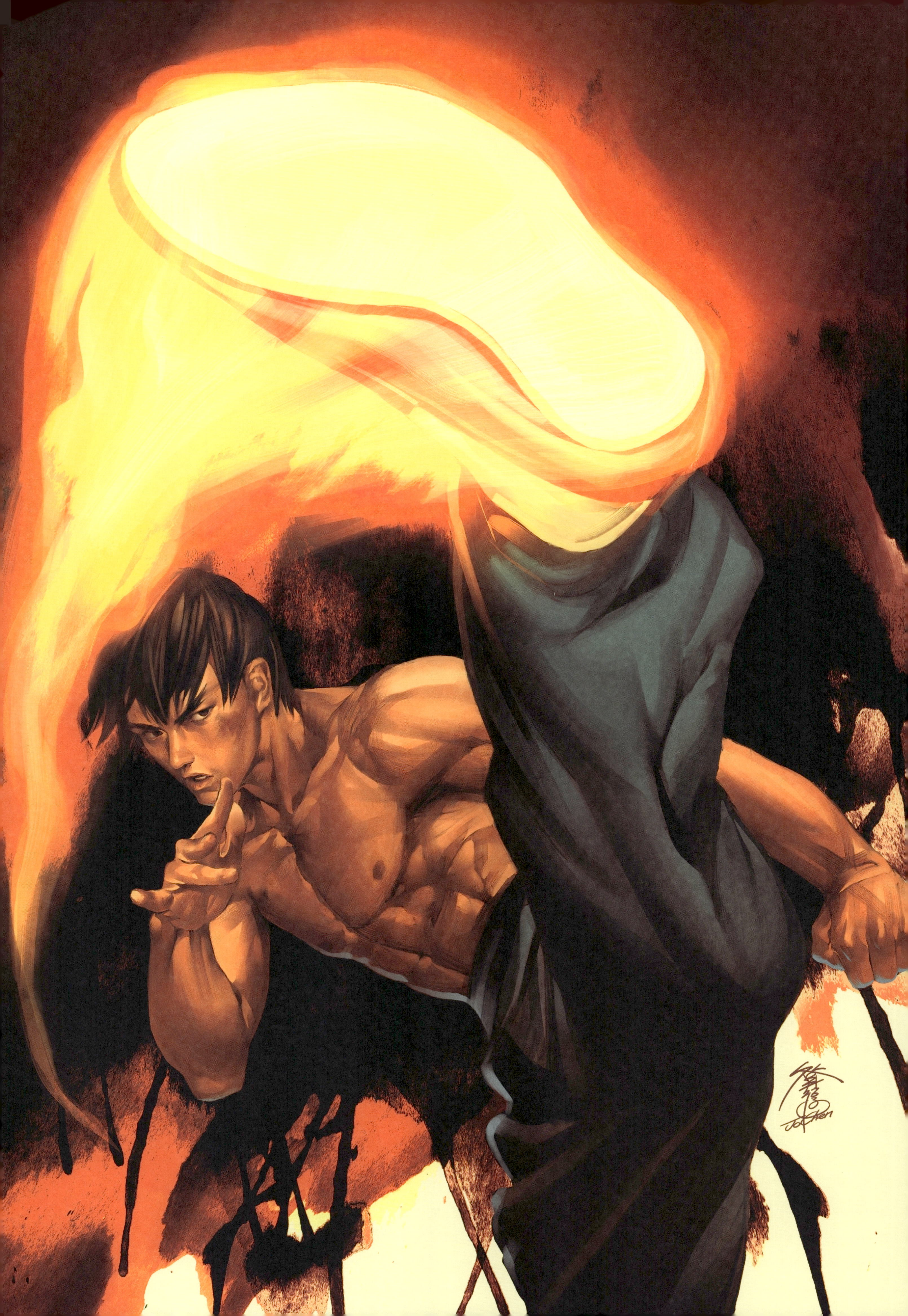

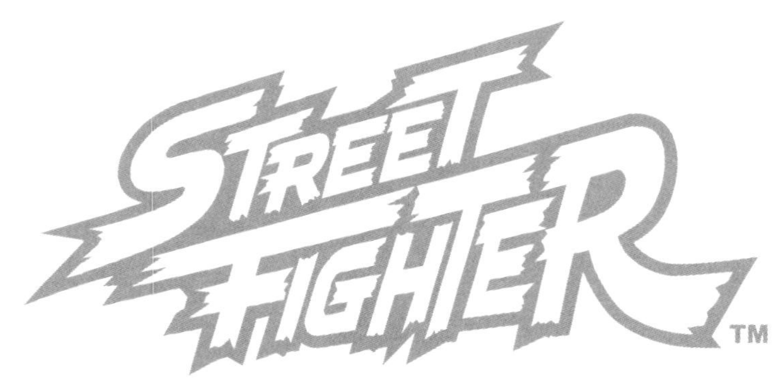

STREET FIGHTER™

FEI LONG

ILLUSTRATED BY JO CHEN

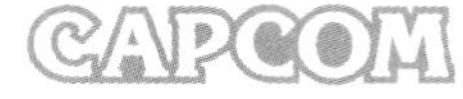

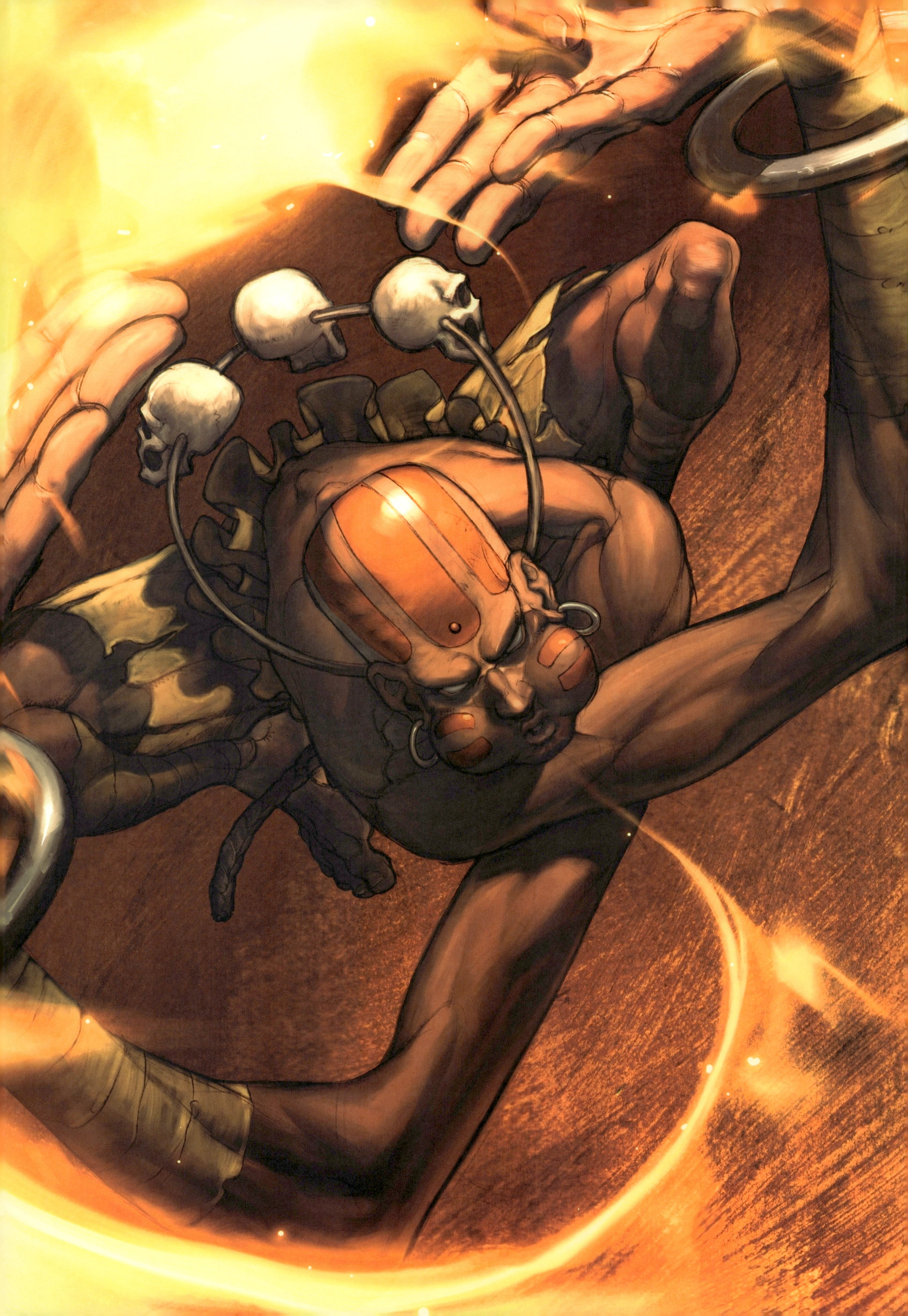

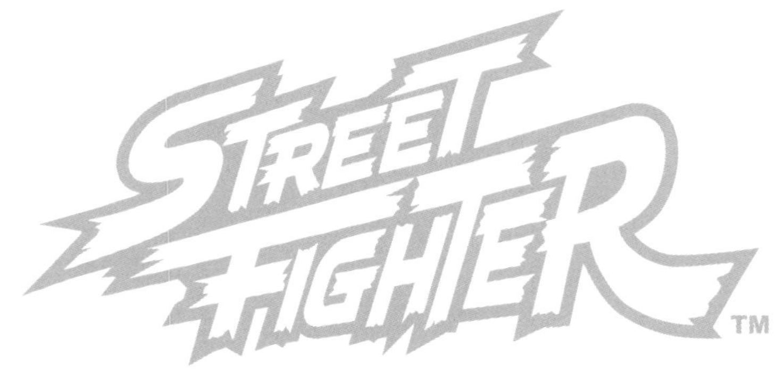

DHALSIM

ILLUSTRATED BY ARNOLD TSANG

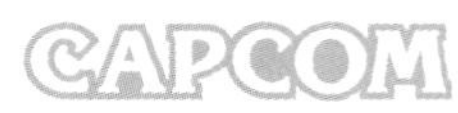

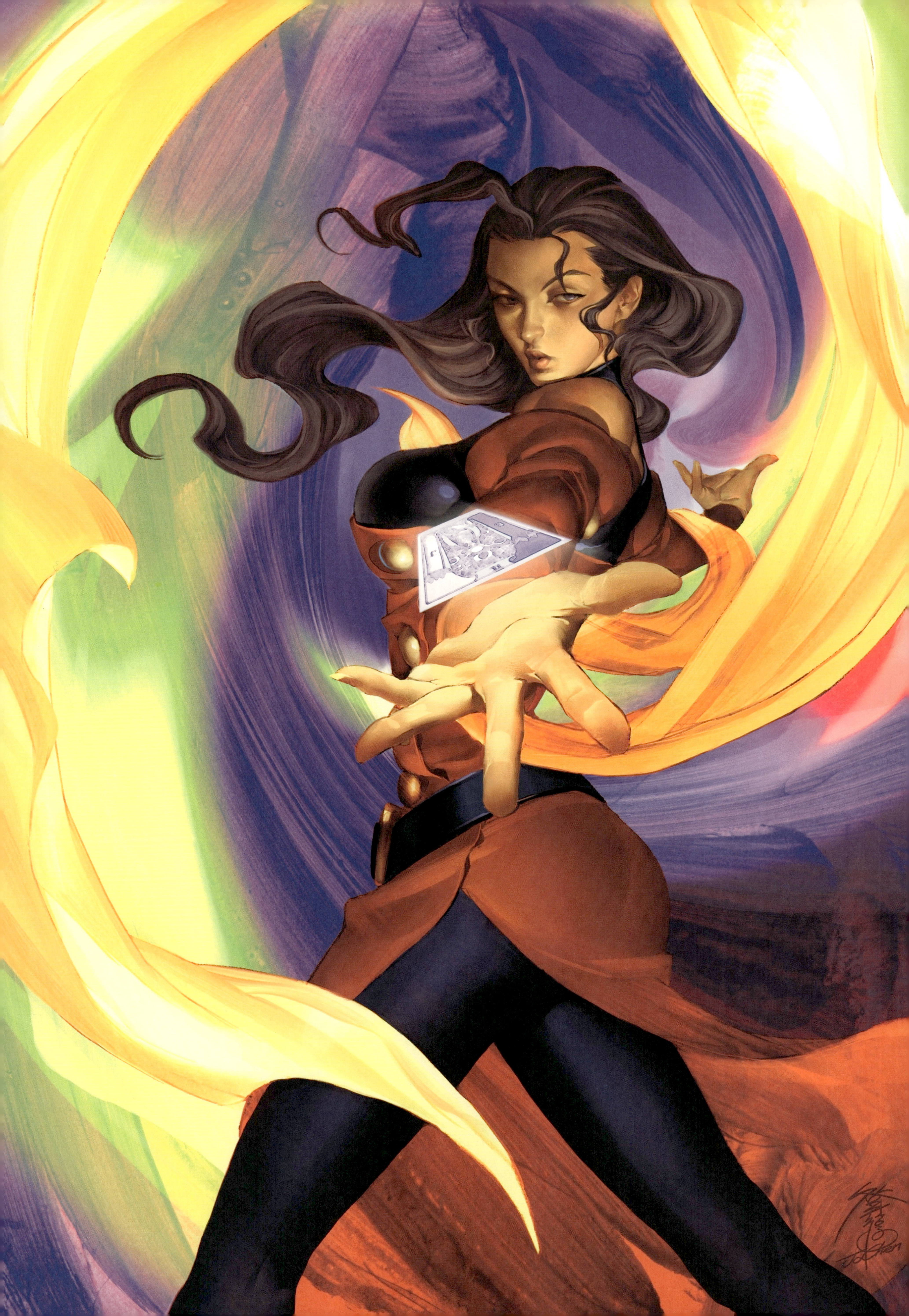

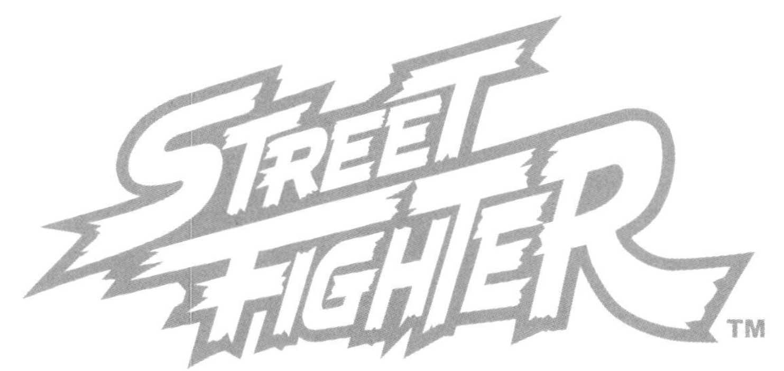

ROSE

ILLUSTRATED BY JO CHEN

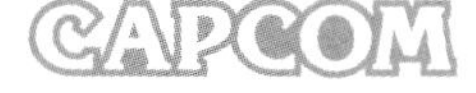

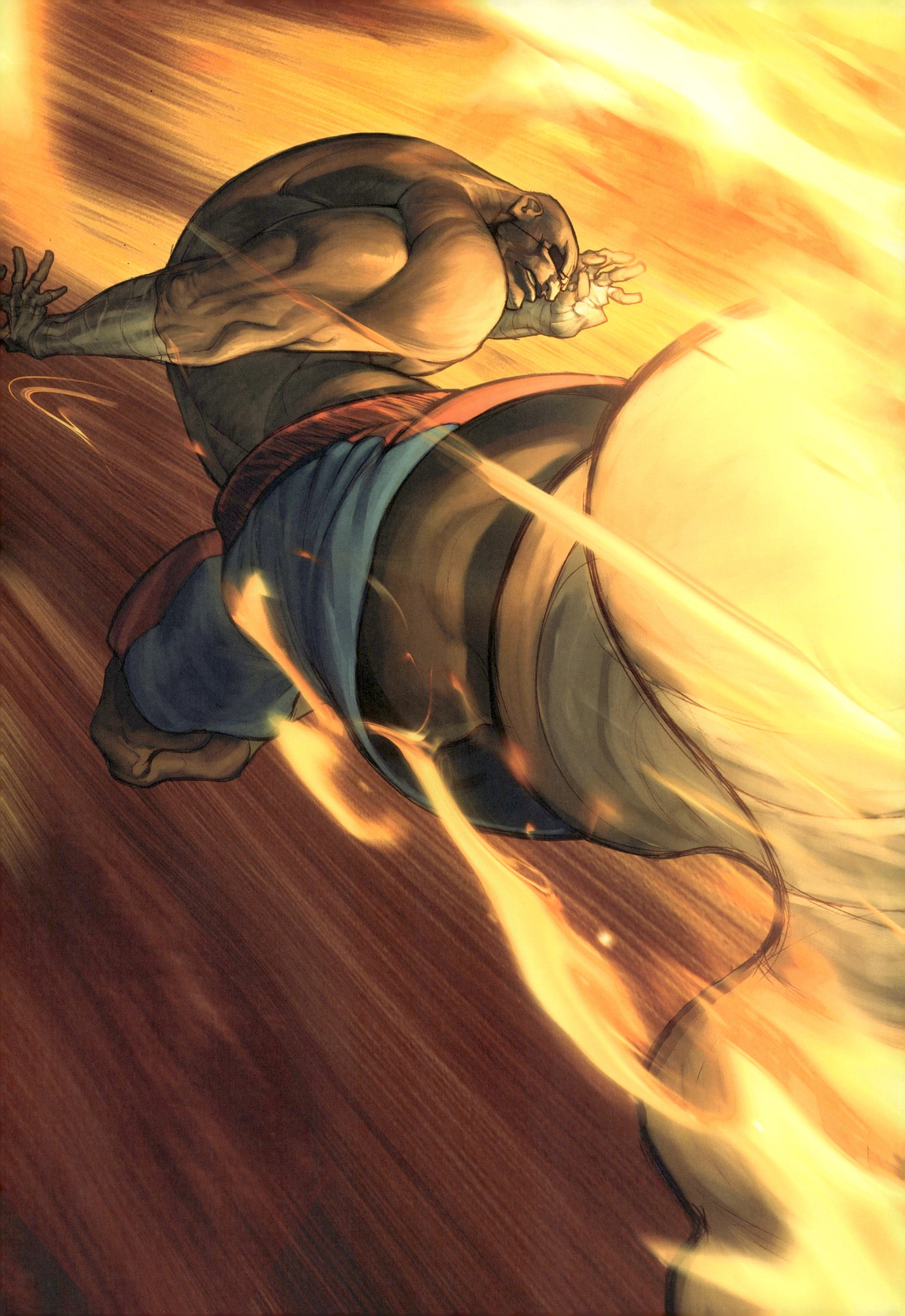

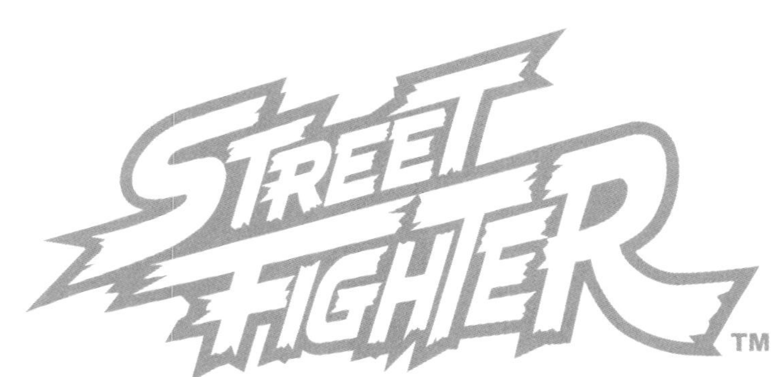

SAGAT

ILLUSTRATED BY ARNOLD TSANG

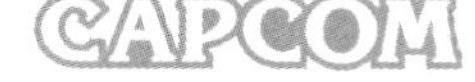

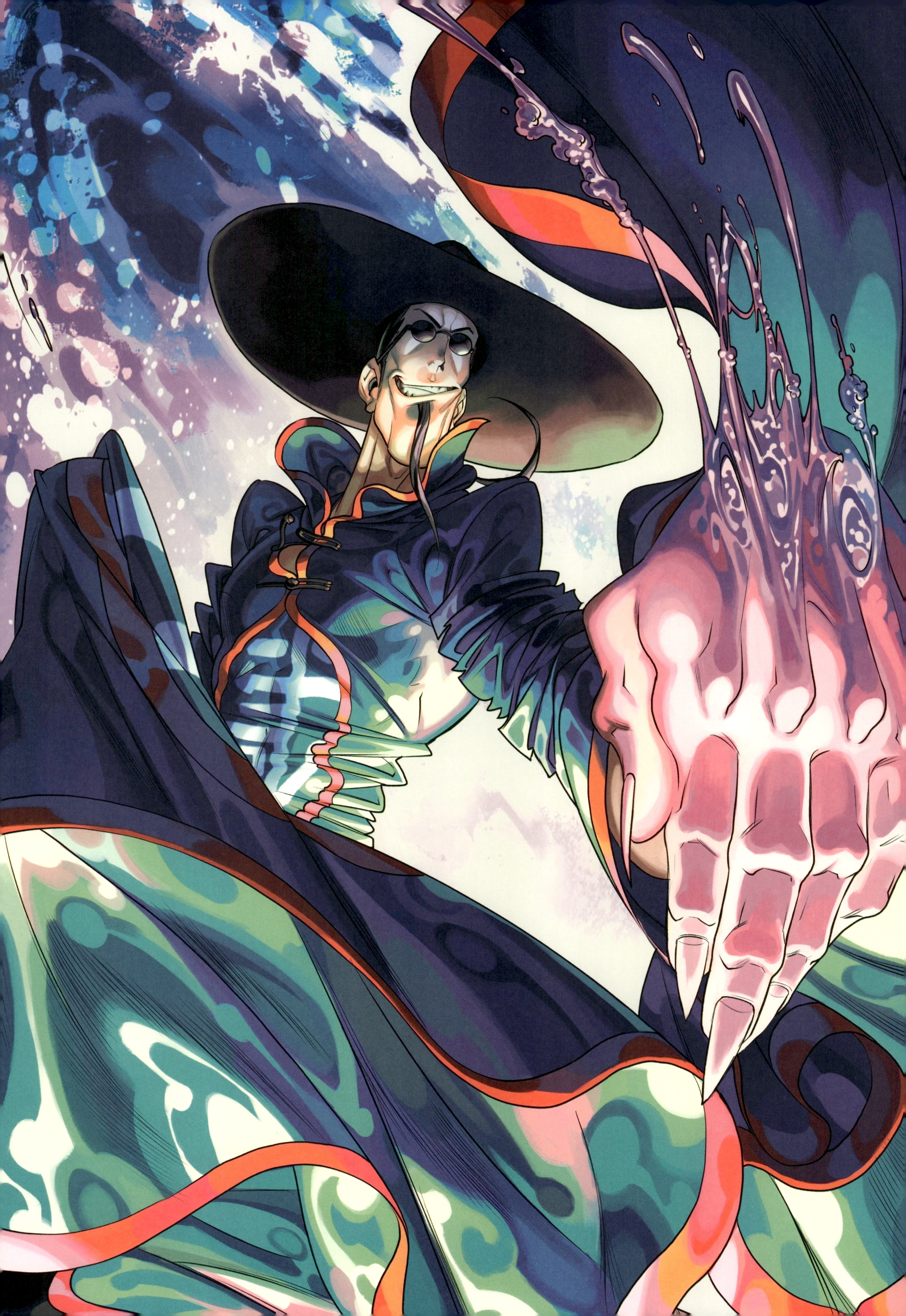

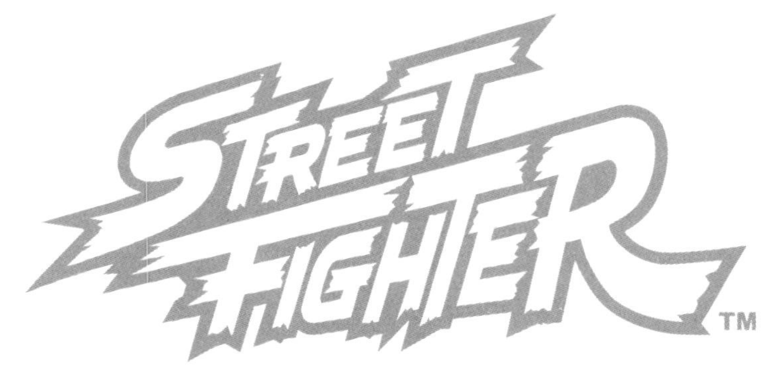

F.A.N.G

ILLUSTRATED BY PANZER

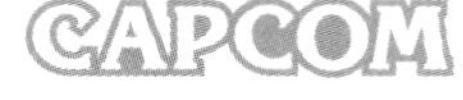

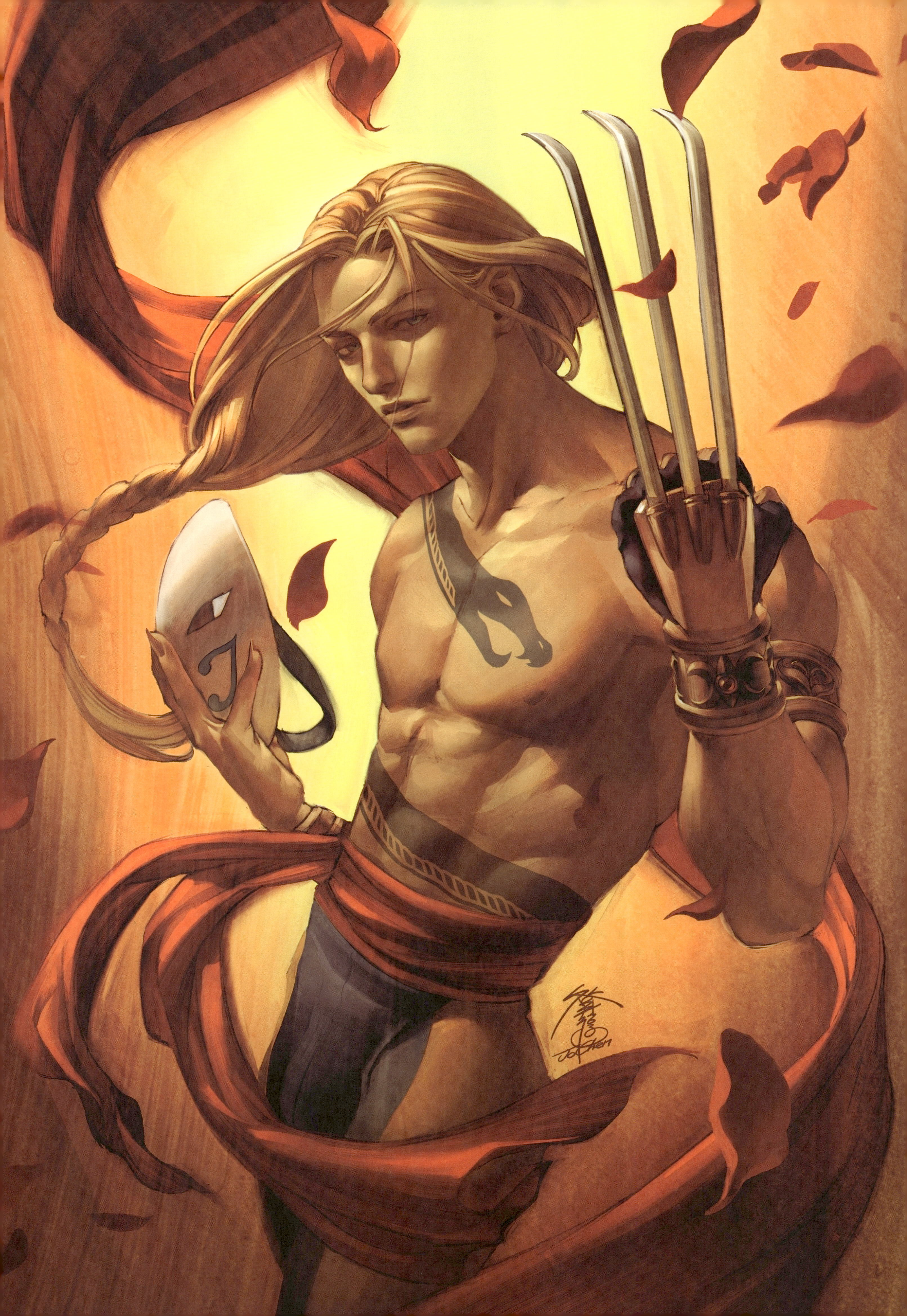

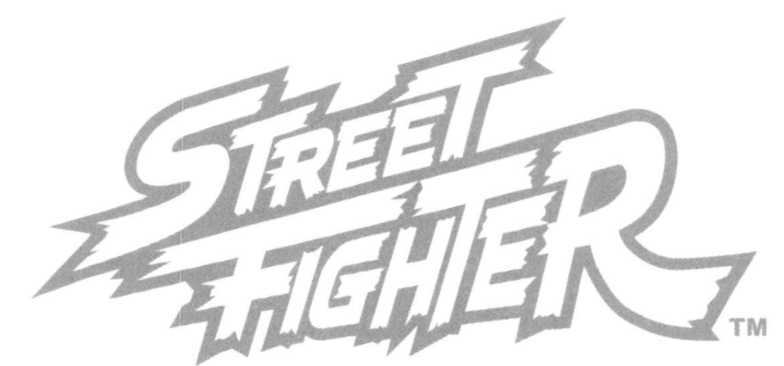

STREET FIGHTER
VEGA
ILLUSTRATED BY JO CHEN

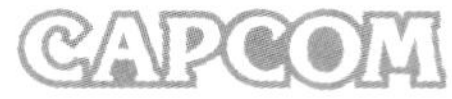

CAPCOM

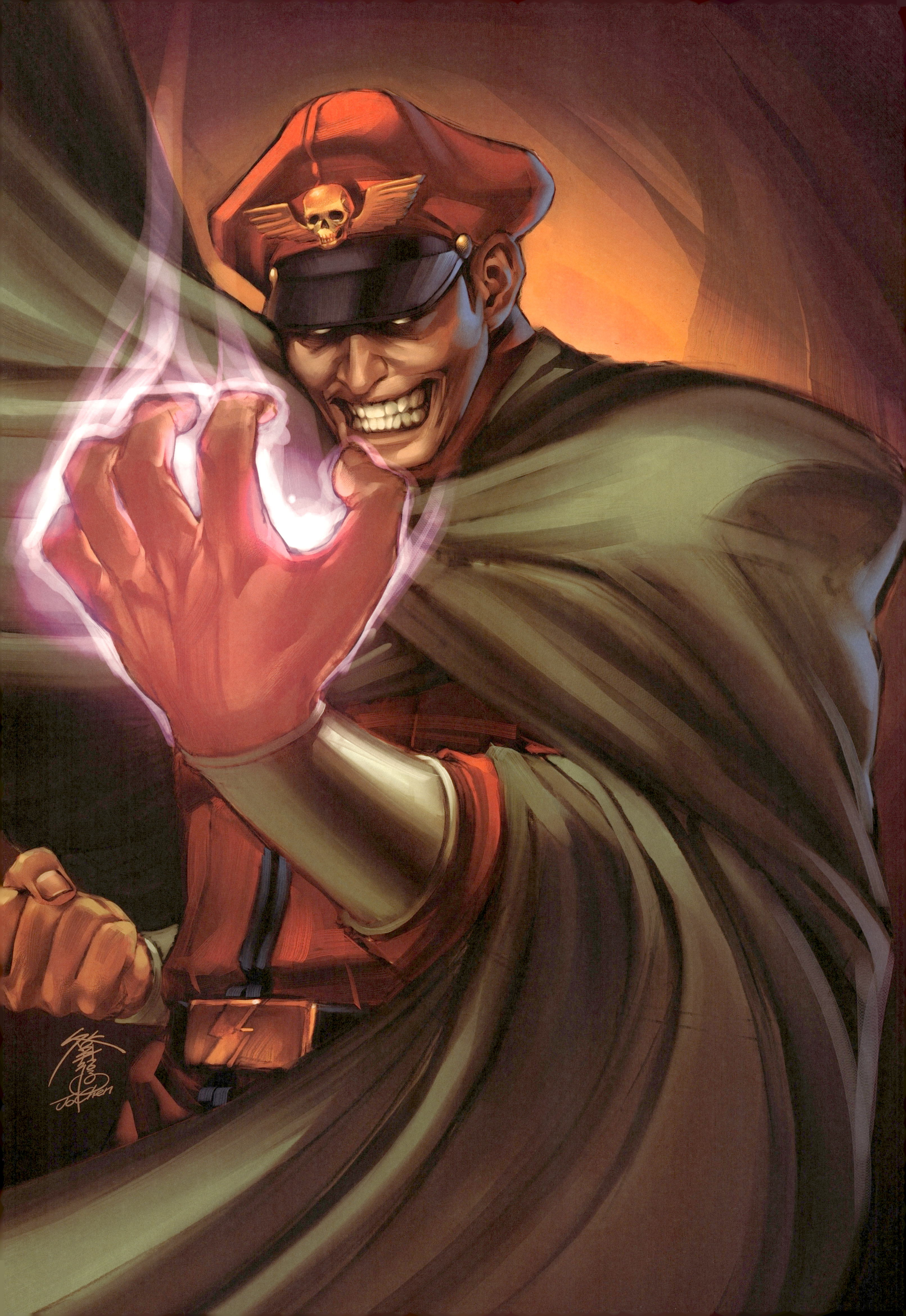

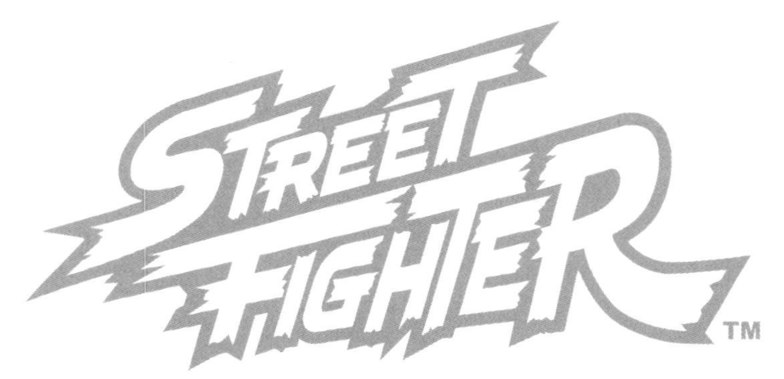

M. BISON

ILLUSTRATED BY JO CHEN

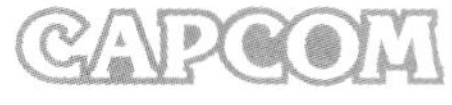

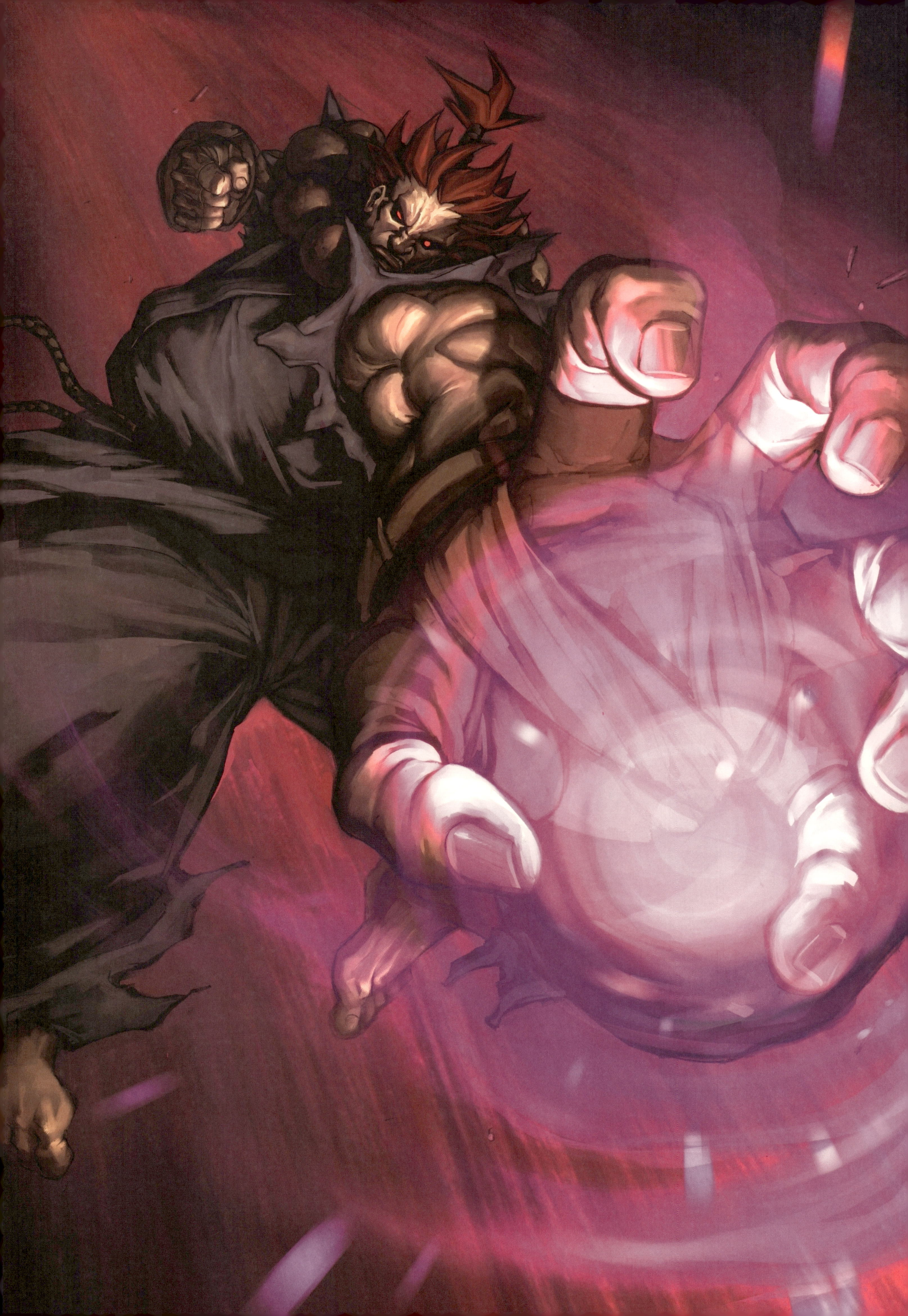

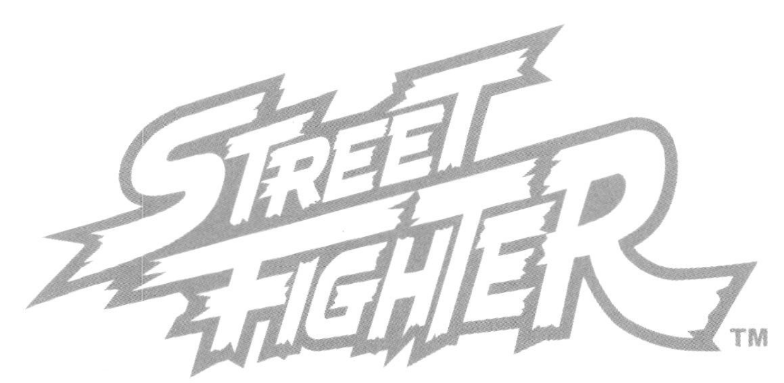

AKUMA

ILLUSTRATED BY ARNOLD TSANG

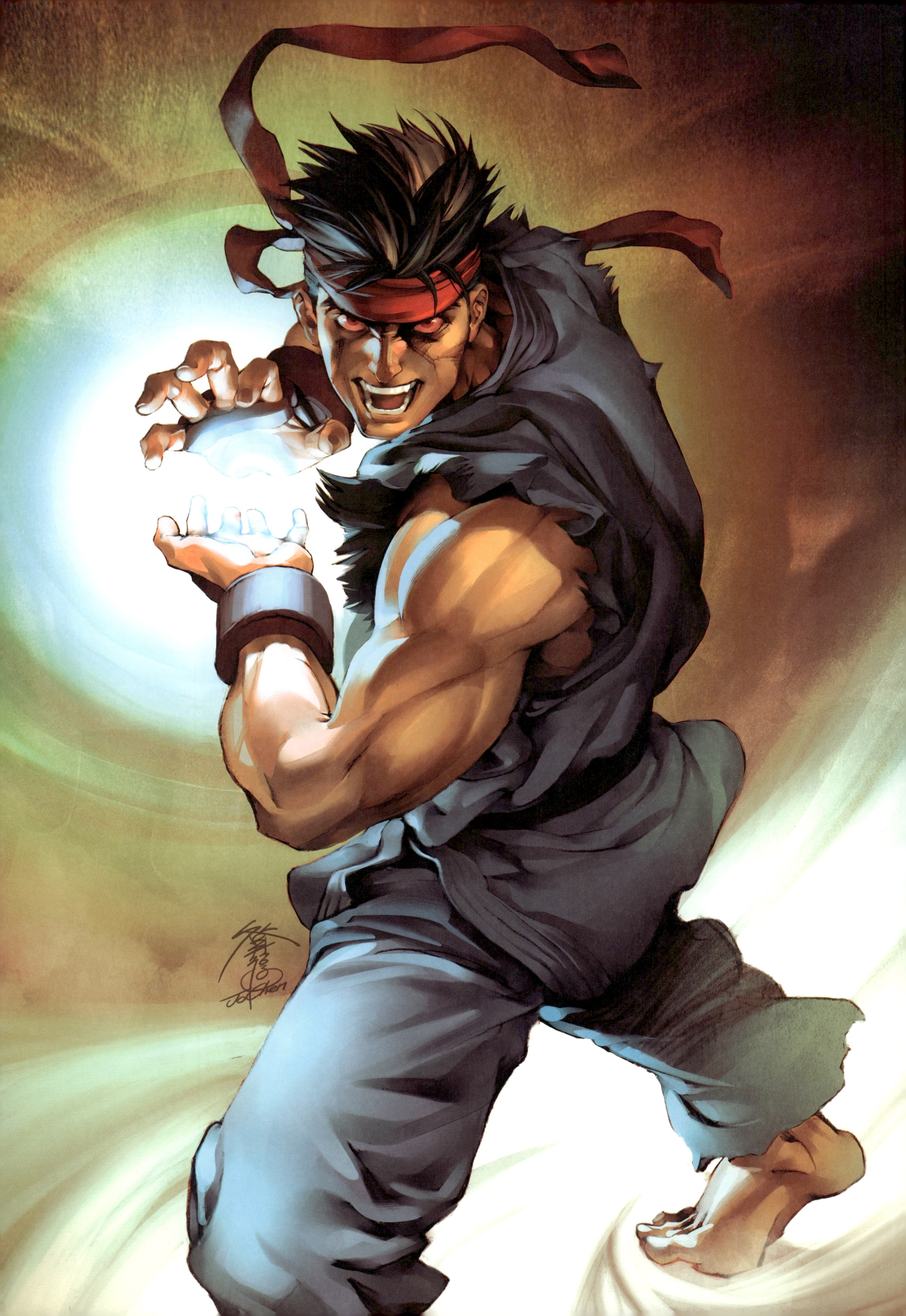

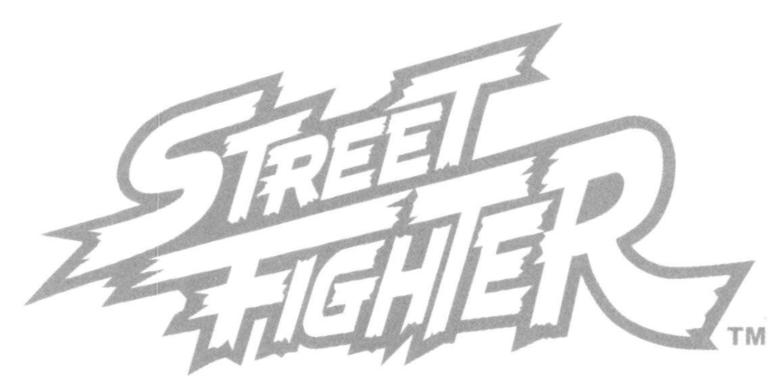

EVIL RYU

ILLUSTRATED BY JO CHEN

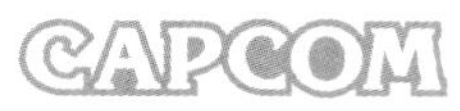